Seashore Life
on Rocky Coasts

JUDITH CONNOR

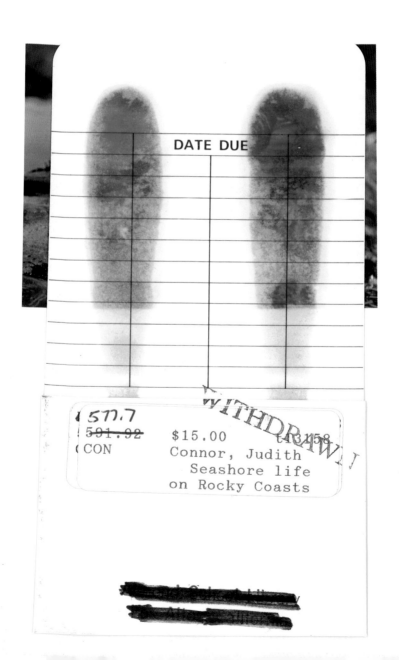

The purpose of the Monterey Bay Aquarium is to stimulate interest, increase knowledge and promote stewardship of Monterey Bay and the world's ocean environment through innovative exhibits, public education and scientific research.

Acknowledgements   I offer humble gratitude to my friends and colleagues who willingly shared their knowledge and helped make this book possible: Chuck Baxter, Rick Brusca, Nora Deans, Mark Denny, Mike Vassar and Steven K. Webster. My special thanks goes to Julie Packard, who steered our course and continues to gently inspire many of us here on Monterey Bay.

This book is dedicated to Professor Kenneth Rinehart, who launched our many trips to rocky coasts around the world, and to Dr. Steven K. Webster, who introduced me to the best of shores at home.

Published in the United States by the Monterey Bay Aquarium Foundation, 886 Cannery Row, Monterey, CA 93940-1085

Library of Congress Cataloging in Publication Data

Connor, Judith, 1948-
Seashore life on rocky coasts / Judith Connor.
p.   cm.—(Monterey Bay Aquarium natural history series)
Includes index.
ISBN 1-878244-05-1 : $9.95
1. Seashore fauna—Juvenile literature. 2. Intertidal fauna—Juvenile literature. I. Title. II. Series.
QL122.2.C655 1993
591.5'2638—dc20   92-42249   CIP

Photo and Illustration Credits:

Cover: Dugald Stermer

Balthis, Frank S.: 4, 60 (top left)

Blake, Tupper Ansel: 31 (top)

Calvin, Jack/Reprinted from *Between Pacific Tides,* Fifth Ed. by Edward F. Ricketts, Jack Calvin & Joel W. Hedgpeth; w/ permission of the publishers, Stanford Univ. Press. © 1985 by the Board of Trustees of Leland Stanford Jr. Univ.: 61 (bottom)

Caudle, Ann: 39 (top), 44 (top), 52 (middle), 59 (top)

Cavagnaro, David: 23 (top)

Chamberlain, Marc C.: 51 (top)

Clevenger, Ralph/ Westlight: 21, 28, 49

Cody, W./Westlight: 27 (bottom), 30

Conlin, Mark/HHP: 51 (bottom)

Foott, Jeff: 1, 7, 9, 12, 13 (bottom), 14 (top), 15, 19 (middle), 22, 25 (top left), 27 (top), 31 (bottom), 33, 34 (bottom right), 40, 43, 47 (top), 52 (top right), 53 (top), 54 (middle), 55 (top), 56 (top), 62 (top), 63

Gohier, Francois: 60 (middle)

Gotshall, Daniel W.: 34 (top left)

Hall, Howard/HHP: 54 (top)

Herrmann, Richard: 23 (middle), 34 (top right), 47 (bottom), 62 (bottom)

Kerstitch, Alex: 38

Langstroth, Libby and Lovell: 45

Monterey Bay Aquarium: 6, 13 (top)

Noonan, Robert: 35 (bottom right), 59 (bottom)

Ormsby, Lawrence: 10-11, 36-37

Rand, Milton/Tom Stack & Assoc.: 8

Rigsby, Michael: 14 (bottom), 18, 19 (bottom), 24, 29 (top), 32, 48 (bottom)

Robinson, George A./Dept. of Special Collections,

Stanford Univ. Libraries: 61 (top)

Sea Studios: 25 (top right)

Snyderman, Marty: 34 (bottom left), 60 (top right)

Sorensen, John: 52 (top left)

Thompson, Frances: 29 (bottom), 35 (top), 44 (middle), 48 (top), 55 (middle), 56 (middle)

Webster, Steven K.: 5, 16-17, 35 (bottom left), 39 (bottom), 44 (bottom), 57

Westmorland, F. Stuart/ Tom Stack & Assoc.: 46

Wrobel, David J.: cover (art reference), 41 (bottom), 53 (bottom)

Wu, Norbert: 41 (top)

Series and Book Editor: Nora L. Deans
Designer: James Stockton, James Stockton & Associates
Printed on recycled paper in Singapore through Interprint, Petaluma, California

CONTENTS

Early morning sunlight filtering through the fog reveals large swells sweeping in toward shore. Pounding waves beat against the rocks, kicking up a froth of agitation. Sea spray adds its salty tang to the air. You can practically taste the excitement in this violent meeting of land and sea and air.

Twice each day the tide ebbs, restraining the reach of the waves and splash. As seething waters recede from shore, distinct bands of sea life appear. Each of these concentrated slices of life is an intertidal community of animals and plants—a region rich with dramatic stories of survival. The retreating tide unveils the drama, introducing a cast of hundreds of intertidal creatures, some living at the highest reach of sea spray, others deep in tide pools.

Bend down. Look closely to discover the communities that dwell in each domain. Meet the creatures one by one; share their stories of survival. Learn how they face the physical challenges of living sometimes in air, sometimes in water. Imagine living with them on a rock, where space is often in short supply and hungry predators abound. Experience life on a rocky shore, an ongoing saga of competing, mating, eating and being eaten.

The hours pass; the sea reclaims what it briefly abandoned. As the rocky shore slips from view below the waves, carry away with you a new sense of wonder and appreciation for the forces that govern life between the tides.

1

ROCKY SHORES

Walk a rocky shore at high tide and you'll miss treasures hidden beneath the waves—the teeming stripes of life that are only slowly revealed as the tide eases out, like a deliberate river in reverse.

From the highest reaches of the ocean spray, down slippery, sloping rocks into deep tide pools and protected crevices, life on the rocky shore segregates into distinct intertidal regions. Positioned by their tolerance and tenacity and by encounters with each other, snails, seaweeds and other creatures align themselves in horizontal bands. Each seashore plant and animal must cope with the comings and goings of the tides, pounding waves and scouring sand.

For the most part, intertidal plants and animals have evolved from ancestors that were tolerant of some of the physical demands of life on land. Like the animals able to survive in fresher water that moved up into estuaries, some seashore species can stand exposure to air better than others. Those that can handle long hours out of the water commonly live higher up on the rocky shore than more sensitive types.

Watch the rocks closely as the tide ebbs, and you'll see each stripe exposed in sequence. In time, you'll come to recognize the features of each stripe and the characters who live there. But to really know the rocky shores is to understand the laws that govern life between the tides.

At low tide, when the shore is exposed, you'll find marine creatures left high and dry. Then the tide rushes in, sweeping over the seaweeds and animals that cling to the rocks. Cool, rich waters revive them: anemones open like flowers, seaweeds bend and sway and barnacles unfurl their feathery legs.

Life begins anew with the incoming tide, but the struggle to survive is unending. Storms roll in without warning to assault the shoreline with tons of crashing water. Sand carried by the waves scrapes and scratches the living residents, or smothers them under a blanket of sediment. The plants and animals fixed to the rocks must endure life in air as well as the physical drag of life in moving water. They must tolerate the shifts from sea to air and back again.

TIDES As vital as a heartbeat, the ebb and flow of tides, more than anything else, sets the pattern of life along rocky coasts. Tides, the regular daily rise and fall of the water along the ocean's shore, help shape rocky shore communities.

Three major forces cause the tides. The moon exerts the greatest pull, dragging out a tidal bulge of water on the moonward

Low tide reveals living treasures to tide pool explorers. At high tide, the seaweeds and animals are once again hidden below the waves.

side of the Earth. On the other side of the Earth, a bulge occurs because the pull of the moon on the water there is less, while the Earth itself is pulled more strongly toward the moon. It takes the Earth 24 hours to complete one rotation on its axis. Moving in the same direction as the Earth's rotation but at a much slower pace, the moon orbits the Earth. The moon's slower orbit around the Earth means the Earth must go a bit farther than one revolution to return to its starting position under the moon. So the daily tidal cycle is a bit longer than a day; it's 24 hours and 50 minutes long.

The sun's gravity also affects the tides. But because the sun is so far away, it pulls with only about half the moon's force.

These two bulges on opposite sides of the Earth are like two giant waves of water that travel across our seas. They cause the world's high tides, while the low-water troughs between them cause low tides. As the Earth rotates under these giant waves, those of us on dry land see the fluid bulges come and go as tides.

Any given spot on the seafloor rotates beneath the two tidal bulges daily, while every shore experiences its own peculiar pattern of tides depending on its location and the shape of its coastline. The California coast has a classic tidal cycle. There are two high tides daily, one usually more extreme than the other—a mixed semi-diurnal pattern.

In some seas, like the English Channel, the greater of the two daily tides can hardly be distinguished, so each day's high tides seem equal. Other basins, like the South China Sea, accentuate the differences between high tides so much that there seems to be only one tide a day.

Green algae on beach rocks along the Oregon coast are exposed to air during calm low tides.

LIFE ON THE ROCKS Crashing waves mark the meeting place of the sea and the Earth's hardened mineral crust we know as land. Life that survives here, on the rocks, depends more on the shape of the shoreline than on the type of rock making up this boundary. The coastal topography and how the shoreline faces out to sea determine, in part, what grows on the rocks and where it grows. You'll see steep, vertical cliffs wearing tight stripes of barnacles and seaweeds, while life on gently sloping beach rock spreads out in broader bands. High up on the wave-splashed reaches of a rock's seaward face, small robust seaweeds thrive. More vulnerable creatures cling to crevices on that same rock's shoreward face.

Middle-sized rocks make the best homes. They usually stay put, allowing seaweeds to become established, but powerful waves tumble them enough to keep any one type of seaweed from taking over. For their size, they bear an amazing bounty of lots of different kinds of plants.

A bigger rock may wear a heavy cover, but it's often a monotonous field of just one or two types of seaweeds. Large boulders have more stability and space, but when a domineering species gains a foothold here, it'll crowd out all the competition.

Fields of smaller, rounded cobblestones that turn and tumble when the surf is high offer temporary homes for delicate, short-lived seaweeds. Further down the scale, little stones are nearly barren seascapes. Storm waves often lift these small stones, turning them into deadly water-borne missiles that smash and devastate creatures living on larger rocks.

Some rocky shorelines sport bands of soft, sedimentary rocks, like shale and sandstone, which split and crumble as they weather. But while they last, these soft rocks offer surfaces for attachment or burrowing possibilities for animals that hide for a living. Some porous rocks retain moisture even at low tide—a boon to their intertidal residents.

On some shores you'll find rugged outcrops of hard granite or basalt that are slow to erode. These igneous rocks are enduring, and it's difficult to hollow out a home inside them. They weather slowly into smooth, stable shapes where marine plants and animals can securely attach.

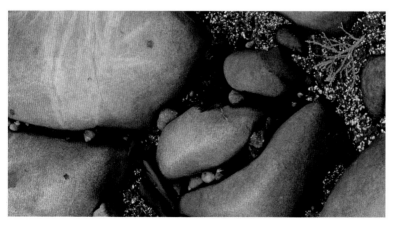

Few animals can survive the agitation of life on small stones tossed around by waves and surf, so these rolling stones are nearly bare.

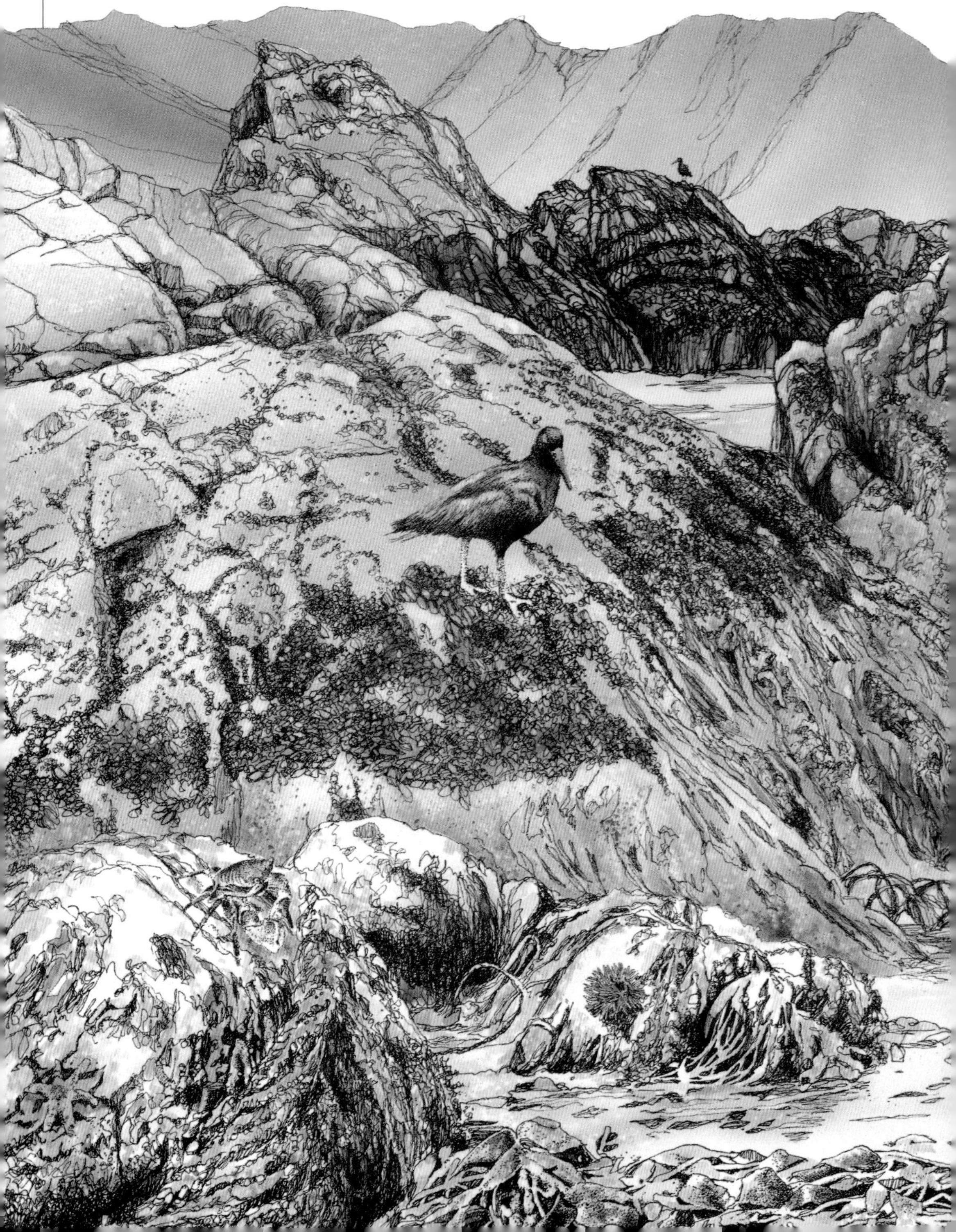

Distinct bands of life mark rocky coasts, from the sparsely populated, highest, driest region up on the rocks to the densely crowded jumble of seaweeds at the water's edge.

SAND A blast of sandy water against the rocky shore can be as abrasive as a bout with an electric grinder, and the steady scrape of sand-laden water can cause the toughest seaweed to surrender. Gritty sand wounds and bruises seashore creatures and scours encrusted rocks clean.

Storm waves tear seaweeds from the rocks and toss them ashore as piles of beach wrack.

In summer, sand brought in by waves builds up beaches and buries rocks. Winter storms remove the sand, liberating the rocks again. These shifting sands act like a wet blanket on low-lying life, smothering sensitive species. A few robust sea creatures, like aggregating anemones and some tolerant red seaweeds, sit out seasonal burials for months, then rapidly recuperate when the sand is washed away.

CLIMATE The local climate, coupled with the rhythm of the tides and the topography of the area, has a profound influence on the survival of sea life along rocky shores. A morning low tide shrouded in cool fog keeps rocky creatures moist, while a midday low tide on a hot sunny day overheats and bleaches plants and dries out animals exposed to the air. Just how hot do they get? At low tide, the temperature of a mussel exposed to sunny, dry air can rise above 80°F, then plunge nearly thirty degrees in half an hour, when the tide comes back in. Some shallow tide pools get even hotter.

Intertidal creatures can't anticipate precisely how physical conditions in their environment will change on any given day. The height of each high tide and its hour of arrival shifts during the year, but the timing of the tides isn't entirely mysterious. Tide tables represent predictions of these changing water levels, although the tides don't function by themselves. Weather conditions undermine the best forecasts of the tides. Changes in atmospheric pressure can change local sea levels. A high pressure system lowers the ocean's level; low pressure elevates it. Winds and storms extend the reach of waves along the shoreline. At low tide, an extra two-foot upsurge added to a wave can bring a refreshing splash of sea water to creatures that might otherwise be stranded high and dry.

The plants and animals that ornament our rocky coasts must survive extremes of climate as well as drastic changes in their surroundings. When chilling waves sweep over sun-baked rocks, temperatures plunge radically from simmering to numbing cold. In some climates, intertidal rocks are exposed to freezing temperatures and grating ice in winter. And drying winds steal life's precious liquid from seashore creatures, while the sun does triple damage: heating up, drying out and burning with its ultraviolet radiation.

Small, isolated tide pools taste the briny extremes of life, from the concentrated saltiness caused by evaporation to the brackishness resulting from fresh water after heavy rains.

Where seabirds congregate, a white patina of guano encrusts the rocks, building up in such high concentrations that these natural fertilizers burn off seaweeds trying to grow there. Higher up on other rocks, seaweeds suffer from a lack of water and vital nutrients when the tide is out, so they don't grow very big on the highest parts of the shore.

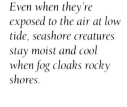

Even when they're exposed to the air at low tide, seashore creatures stay moist and cool when fog cloaks rocky shores.

Where seabirds gather, the rocks are coated with guano, which burns off seaweeds before they can grow.

THE STRIPES OF LIFE

Each horizontal stripe on a rocky coast marks the home site of specific plants and animals. What determines which creatures live in a particular stripe? Their survival depends on their abilities to withstand the physical stress and biological interactions in that location.

The highest band harbors small, drab-looking creatures that face the worst extremes of life between the tides. Tiny, dark snails perch in rocky crevices. Gray barnacles and wiry turfs of nailbrush seaweed roughen rocks at the high reaches of the waves. Slender marine relatives of pillbugs race for cover, while lively rock crabs dance across the rocks in the lulls between the waves.

Creatures adapted to survive bright sunlight, dehydration and rapid changes in temperature find plenty of room here in the sparsely settled stripes high on the rocky

The zones of life on a rocky shore range from the highest, driest zone on rocks barely washed by wave splash (right), to wetter tide pools (below), to seaweed-choked rocks at the water's edge (far right).

shore. At high tide, they soak up life-giving fluids from the cool water that surrounds them. At low tide, the sun and wind can overheat them and leave them high and dry.

In the next lower band, rockweeds appear in an orderly vertical progression: first as olive-colored stubs, then little branching plants which sprout, in turn, over a dangling growth of seaweeds. The vegetation droops as the tide abandons it, betraying limpets and other creatures that were concealed among the seaweeds. Like plants on land, seaweeds have a special set of requirements that dictates where they end up. Seaweeds depend on sunlight to fuel the production of their carbohydrate food supply. Too little light stunts their growth. Too much damages their delicate internal machinery and bleaches the life out of them.

The tide sinks to its lowest ebb, divulging further secrets. A curtain of green surf grass separates, exposing a flash of light-bulb tunicates. A boulder left high and dry above an emerald tide pool serves as a perch for visiting seabirds. A black cormorant flies down and settles there, stretching out its wings to dry. A tangle of leathery kelps streams from the tide pool in a good-bye salute to the receding water.

While the more spacious higher stripes face extremes in sunlight, the lower intertidal zones, less frequently exposed to air, are often crowded. Forced to share space, plants and animals interact with one another and influence each other's survival. Some behaviors enhance the survival of a species, like building a nest and guarding it from predators to protect the eggs or growing youngsters.

Other interactions, like competition and predation, pit intertidal creatures against each other. Plants and animals struggle for a piece of the rock to call their own as they grow and reproduce, find food to eat and avoid being eaten. If there isn't enough room or food to go around, natural rivalries develop. A crowd of filter-feeding animals can remove most of the plankton from the surrounding water, leaving nearby filter-feeders without enough food to grow. Two predators may fight over prey, with the battle leading to a meal for one or both, and perhaps a new vacancy on the rock.

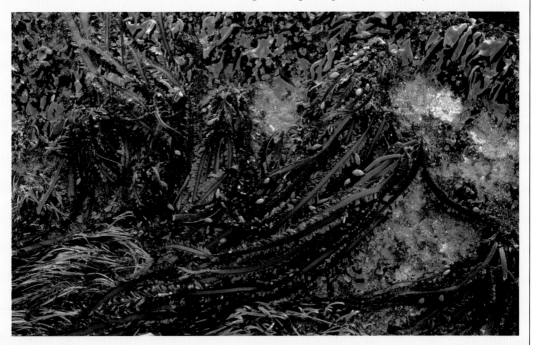

WIND AND WAVES As offshore swells roll in toward land and shallow water, they mount into breaking waves. The waves peak as they move shoreward, growing ever steeper as the flat stretches of water between them shorten. Crest after crest, the waves close ranks, then attack the shore with an urgent, bashing rhythm.

A blustery day adds greater bedlam to the water's movement. Winds heap up peaks atop the swells or blow water off the crests to fashion whitecaps on the waves. During storms, waves assault the shore in random, unpredictable patterns. Three large waves trail a minor one, then a monster slams against the rocks, throwing spray twenty feet into the air.

Series of waves come and go, surging over and between the rocks like reversible rivers. The waves bring food and oxygen to rocky shore animals and carry off their larvae and wastes.

The impact, acceleration and drag of waves exert great physical forces on the rocky shore. The sea launches its best displays of power against open, unprotected coasts, where winds blowing across great stretches of open ocean have built up the energy of the waves. Winds that blow across the thousands of unbroken miles of the Pacific Ocean enlarge the swells advancing toward the California coast. In some spots, these same swells are calmed by barriers that impede their progress, like offshore kelp forests, islands and sheltering coves and harbors.

Rocky shore creatures must constantly deal with the drag and shock of waves on these violent shores. Those that survive the waves' violence are often flexible or small and strong. Encrusting creatures, like bryozoans and crustose coralline algae, live flat against the rocks and so they feel less drag from the waves.

Waves carry oxygen and food to rocky shore animals, and transport their offspring and wastes to other places.

Some seaweeds on the rocky shore, like tiny Turkish towels (*Mastocarpus* spp.), survive in all kinds of situations, from rocks in sheltered coves to wave-washed open coasts. But waves are more likely to remove large animals than small ones from the rocky shore.

Flexible creatures like seaweeds can actually grow quite large on wave-swept rocks. Feather boa kelp (*Egregia menziesii*) and oarweeds (*Laminaria* spp.) for example, dance limp and elastic in the waves. They stream out from their holdfasts with the flow, only to whip back in again. If you look closely, you might see small limpets that spend their entire lives aboard these kelps. They protect their flat snail-like bodies with streamlined shells, three times as long as they are wide. The shape of their shells cuts down the water's pull, and to minimize the drag even more, the limpets will re-orient themselves so that they face the least resistance.

Limpets aren't alone in their ability to withstand life in the waves. Mussels (*Mytilus* spp.) dwell in crowded colonies, densely packed in among others of their kind. Each mussel lives within two hinged, streamlined shells that can withstand the force of waves. The bumpy shape of a closely packed mussel bed changes the flow of water over its rock in ways that are both positive and negative to

Curtains of red Turkish towel seaweed and carpets of green surf grass survive in many different sites, from quiet coves to open coasts.

the mussels. While the difference in water pressure in the bed and out in the mainstream encourages water movement through the mussel bed, it pulls up on the mussels too, and strains their ties to home. But strong threads of hardened glue firmly attach each mussel to its rock. To slowly change position, the mussel loosens old threads and makes new ones. Some mussels lay down more threads as winter approaches to increase their chances of surviving forceful seasonal storm waves.

TURBULENT MIXING   Throughout the seasons, the turbulence of wave-washed sites both makes life possible and threatens its existence. All rocky shore creatures depend on waves to renew supplies of clean water, oxygen, carbon dioxide and nutrients. Filter-feeding animals, like mussels and barnacles, rely on water motion to carry in new food supplies and carry off their wastes. Water movement also helps carry offspring away from their parents' territory. Sometimes it plays a role in promoting safe, successful sex. Gentle water motion helps mix eggs and sperm together, but where it's very turbulent, eggs and sperm don't get the chance to make the necessary contact with each other.

Sea palms (top) live near mussels and goose barnacles (bottom) on cold, wave-washed Pacific coasts. The goose barnacles and mussels face the waves with hard, streamlined shells packed together in tight crowds. The sea palms stand upright and flexible, bouncing back after each wave.

2

THE SPLASH ZONE

A surge of water bathes the rocks, then drains off the highest, driest stripe of intertidal life. This zone, wetted only by sea spray and an occasional wave splash, is more land than sea. The rocks look bare or are etched with the rust-colored stains of lichens and microscopic algae. Animals in the spray zone tend to be small and hard to see. Most survive the long low tides by enclosing themselves in tight shells to keep from drying out. Some simply move on to wetter pastures.

PAINTED ROCKS High in the spray zone, rocks are slick with microscopic life. Invisible threads of marine bacteria wrapped in gelatinous envelopes leave telltale slippery, blackened stains. And countless diatoms, like tiny jewels in iridescent opal cases, adhere to the rocks, giving the splash zone a patina of weathered mahogany. Diatoms are actually microscopic plants. Like other ocean plants, they draw their life from the water that surrounds them. Absorbing water, carbon dioxide and other chemicals from the sea, diatoms capture the sun's energy to convert them into sugars, amino acids and other seaweed building blocks. This remarkable act, called photosynthesis, sustains plants and forms the basis of the food webs that support almost all living creatures on our planet. Diatoms perform this vital role with style, displaying an astounding variety of textures, shapes and sizes.

PATCHES OF BARNACLES It may look quiet here, but subtle stories of life and death are playing out on the rocks. As the sea splashes the painted rocks, it wets a chalky, honeycomblike patch of barnacles. Instantly, acorn barnacles (*Chthamalus* and *Balanus* spp.) fling open the trap doors of their shells. In unison, they kick their wispy, jointed legs into the sea water that carries oxygen and bits of food.

One of the acorn barnacles in the patch extends its slender tubelike penis from its shell. Two years old and nearly half an inch across, this young adult is ripe for reproduction. With its penis, the barnacle explores a two-inch circle of the neighborhood. It probes another barnacle; this one has found a mate. The two barnacles are hermaphrodites, each having male and female sexual organs. Both can make eggs and sperm, but they still need to breed together. The first barnacle pumps sperm through its penis into its neighbor's shell where 500 eggs are ready. For now, the neighbor will play mother and produce a brood of young. Next time, it may take on the role of father and send its sperm to another barnacle.

*Where waves splash high
on the rocks, small
barnacles form rough
colonies.*

Meanwhile, the next generations ride the waves in close to shore. The sea splash carries larvae, including young barnacles, to the barnacle patch. A barnacle larva lands on the rock and with its antennae explores for the perfect perch. Sensing a delicate, familiar chemical trace coming from adult acorn barnacles, it settles there. Gluing its head down to the spot, it starts to make itself a shell.

This newcomer doesn't concern the older barnacles. They don't miss a beat while water's around. Whipping its legs back and forth through the spray, each barnacle kicks tiny plants and animals into its mouth hidden inside its shell.

Green sea lettuce is a true weed. Growing quickly in salty puddles and shallow pools, it matures and produces spores before most algae.

SPLASH POOLS Near the barnacles, shallow basins worn into the rocks collect and mix rain and ocean spray. Hot, dry weather evaporates the puddles, making them saltier than the sea. Later, heavy rains dilute them until they're nearly fresh. Creatures that survive in splash pools must tolerate the stress of both extremes.

Green seaweeds (*Enteromorpha* spp. and *Ulva* spp.) are among those that call splash pools home. In stringy strands like cellophane noodles, these seaweeds release drops into a splash pool. Each trickle liberates a hundred microscopic swimming cells from the seaweed noodles. The puddles pulse with unseen mating action as the minute swimmers clump with others of their species and pair up. Each twosome fuses into a single swimmer that settles on the basin floor. Then the settlers start to grow into a new patch of green seaweed noodles.

The splash of an ocean wave sends tiny crimson crustaceans called copepods diving for the bottom of the splash pool. When the tide pool regains its calm, the copepods (*Tigriopus* spp.) dart about again, using their special mouthparts to scrape off recent splash pool settlers. The hungry copepods devour most of the fresh green seaweed growth, but a few slender strands escape their notice. Soon these strands will grow into longer streamers that will redress the naked boulders.

DIFFERENT SITES HAVE DIFFERENT STRIPES

All over the earth, from the poles to the equator, rocky shores are marked by stripes of intertidal plant and animal communities. But not all rocky shores look the same. Some bear broad, rich stripes teeming with sea creatures; others have only the barest hint of a band of life.

Many regional factors affect what lives along the shore. Weather, tidal fluctuations, waves and climate all contribute to the differences you see in rocky coasts around the world.

If you travel to cold seas where nutrient-rich waters nourish algal growth, you'll find a rich diversity of animals. In polar seas, ice governs the stripes of life between the tides by scouring seaweeds and animals off the intertidal rocks.

Visit more temperate shores like Washington's Puget Sound and the Bay of Fundy in Maine, and you'll witness enormous tidal changes—ten feet or more—that expose broad stripes of seaweeds and animals. Where forceful waves beat strong and steady, like on the exposed outer coast of Alaska, the stripes of life extend upward to even greater heights.

Along the coasts of the Caribbean Sea and other tropical shorelines, you'll notice

Rocky coasts are found all over the world, from the coast of Maine (top) to the coast of Kauai, Hawaii (above).

very little tidal variation. In areas like this, where there's not much tidal change, the stripes of life are compressed into narrow bands. You'll find familiar forms here—but different species—of coralline algae, anemones, barnacles, snails, crabs and urchins. But the tropics have their own distinctive characters, too, like fire corals and true corals and limestone-laden green algae. Reef-building corals sometimes grow right up to the sea's surface, but they're not true intertidal creatures. When exposed to the air at the lowest of tides, the tips of the corals die back.

SCAVENGERS Between the barnacle patches and splash pools, hundreds of inch-long isopods (*Ligia* spp.) scurry across the rocks. Valuable garbage disposers, these crustaceans scavenge dead plants and animals left to decompose on the shore.

The body of each isopod has bands or segments like its pillbug relatives on land. But the ocean isopod can't roll up into a ball to protect itself. It relies on speed to escape from danger. As it darts over the rocks, an isopod trails two distinctive forked spines from its rear quarters. The spines act as rudders to keep the speeding animal upright.

A dozen isopods back down to the splash pool to dip their spines into the puddle. Each draws water up from its spines to its gills. As long as their gills stay wet, the isopods can explore the higher, drier rocks above. Remoistened now, the crustaceans dash back up to the top of the spray zone.

As the falling tide abandons the spray zone, the highest rocks begin to dry to escape the drying sun and wind. Eventually, the isopods scramble for cracks in the rocks.

PERIWINKLE TRAILS Other creatures hide in the dampness of rocky crevices. Between clusters of barnacles, one snail—a periwinkle (*Littorina* spp.)—wanders high above the waves, sliding on a trail of slime. As it glides along, the snail sticks out its tongue to "lick" the rock that's coated with a film of microscopic plants. The snail's tongue (or radula) has rows of rasping teeth that scrape off plants as the snail advances over the rock.

After the snail has passed, the rock retains a taste of periwinkle essence. Trailing behind the first snail, another periwinkle tracks its kin by scent. Some of these subtle trails may lead hungry snails to greener seaweed pastures. Other trails may help snails locate mates.

As the tide recedes, fewer splashes hit the highest of the rocks. The periwinkles congregate in rocky crevices, each snail secreting a drop of glue to anchor it in place. The glue holds tight so the snail can seal itself up inside its shell to wait for wetter times. One by one, the snails withdraw into their shells and close their doors against the coming intertidal drought. Safe inside their shells, the snails' gills stay wet. Periwinkles can survive for months without really getting wet.

LIMPET FARMERS Other snails, called limpets, glide about beneath cap-shaped shells. Some limpets (*Lottia pelta* and *Acmaea mitra*) wear shells as smooth as ceramic bowls; others wear elaborate shells sculptured with ribs or keyholes. Like periwinkles, limpets are grazers; they scrape algae off the rocks.

Several kinds of limpets maintain gardens. An owl limpet (*Lottia gigantea*) stakes out a farm tract about 13 inches square. The animal guards its farm from all intruders. It shoves its shell like a bulldozer against mussels and anemones that seem too close, forcing them to relocate or, at least, not move in closer.

On patrol of its home patch, the owl limpet bumps into a smaller limpet. It tries to bulldoze the intruder from its garden, but

The owl limpet (below) cleared other limpets from its territory, except one out of reach on its back. Periwinkles (bottom) huddle in a rocky crevice to wait out low tide together.

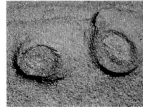

Rockweeds (left) camouflage a half-inch-long isopod of the same color. Two nickel-size limpets (above) nestle in home spots they have worn into the rock.

the invader proves evasive. The small limpet avoids the bulldozer by climbing up on top of its shell. Ignoring its hitchhiker, the owl limpet cruises on, rasping algae off the rocks as it goes.

Because its teeth are capped with iron, the owl limpet can grind right into rock. Over the past months, it has rasped a home scar in the rock—a hollow with the exact dimensions of its shell. After patrolling its farm, the owl limpet retreats to the shallow puddle in its home scar and settles in the perfectly fitted pocket to wait out the low tide.

Other exploring limpets migrate up and down the boulders. Young ones tend to live at lower levels. Older, larger limpets take higher spots along the shore. They carry a small reservoir of water in their shells. Most of those gathered on the high rocks have tall shells that hold quite a bit of liquid; ones that live lower on the shore have lower, flatter shells. The whitecap limpet (*Acmaea mitra*) is one exception to the rule. It wears one of the very tallest shells but lives low on the rocky shore.

Limpet survival takes its tempo from the rhythm of the tides. At high tide, waves stimulate them to move about and search for food. But as the rocks dry with the falling tide, the limpets seek refuge.

Many join periwinkles in rocky crevices in the splash zone, plastering themselves against the boulders to slow evaporation from their bodies. Others chase the falling tide, sliding down the rock face into the next stripe of life where the sea still lingers in the seaweeds.

3

LIVING HIGH AND DRY

Below the desolate spray zone, isolated patches of seaweeds shelter animals too vulnerable to survive on dry, bare rocks. Limpets and other snails snuggle in among the plants, seeking the dampness there. Residents of this high intertidal zone have adapted to living out of water most of the time. High tides wash over them, but low tides leave them high and dry, sometimes for an entire day. Like desert creatures, animals here lie low during dry spells and in the heat of day. They'll scurry into action in the cool dampness of evening or when the tide returns.

ROCKWEED REVELATIONS Limpets flee the drying splash zone higher up, moving down past sprouts of stubby rockweeds to more stately clumps below. Some of these rockweeds (*Pelvetia* spp.) slap the shore with slender branches, while others (*Fucus* and *Hesperophycus* spp.) fling their broader limbs out from their bases. The moplike rockweeds that enfold the limpets also polish the rock surface around them. The rockweeds' flopping action keeps more delicate algae from taking hold nearby, so the rocks stand bare and ready for new rockweeds to colonize.

    The bloated tips of the rockweeds bounce with each wave. The plants dangle in seeming disarray, but there's some order in this mayhem. The rockweeds produce eggs and sperm inside those inflated branches. The bumpy, buoyant branches droop together, so the reproductive parts of different branches end up side by side. Slime oozes from the drying tips—a useful, sexy slime that carries sperm to the eggs where they can mix together. After they're fertilized, the sticky eggs adhere to the rocks. If they survive and grow, they'll start new rockweed generations.

A NEST IN THE ROCKWEEDS New generations of fish also get their start under the rockweeds. A female sculpin (*Clinocottus* spp.) explores a rocky ledge; a male sculpin trails behind her. Mottled green and brown, the sculpins are camouflaged among the plants. With their flat heads and smooth bodies, the fish fit snug against the rocks.

    Heavy with eggs, the female fish pokes around under the rockweeds. In a deep crevice below a clump of weeds, she selects her spawning site. She lays 200 round, brown eggs in a lump as big as a baseball. Her work complete, she swims away, and the male takes over. He wraps himself around the lump to guard the nest and watch his brood. The rockweeds keep the eggs damp while they develop into tiny sculpins.

Rockweed's inflated branch tips (left) conceal its eggs and sperm. Rockweeds share space with barnacles living high and dry on the rocks (below).

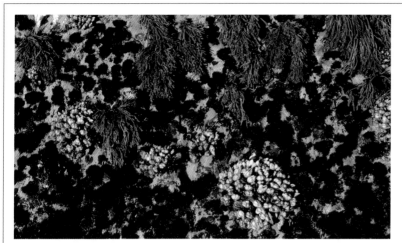

Dark tufts of nailbrush alga grow below the longer rockweeds.

AMONG THE BIGGER BARNACLES Arranged in clusters between the rockweed patches are several kinds of acorn barnacles (*Balanus*, *Chthamalus* and *Tetraclita* spp.). Because these barnacles spend more time under water, they can filter-feed for long intervals each day, so they grow larger than the ones stuck up higher in the spray zone. In places where the barnacles crowd together, the larger ones get pushy and try to enlarge the space they claim as home. They adjust their plates and expand their sites as they grow up and out. Using the edges of their shells, they shove off other creatures that might challenge their positions.

Some creatures defy the sharp-edged shells and claim living space inside the barnacle. Some acorn barnacles reluctantly play host to an internal parasite—the isopod (*Hemioniscus balani*) related to garden pillbugs.

As a youngster in the plankton, the isopod hooks itself onto a copepod. While the copepod drifts with the water currents, it transports the growing isopod. By the time the isopod develops its male reproductive organs, it's big enough to cut loose from the copepod, its first host, and look for its second host, a barnacle. If it finds a barnacle with a female isopod, the unattached male isopod stops to mate. If it finds a barnacle without an isopod to call its own, the male isopod moves right in. There, in its new host, it undergoes an amazing change, transforming from a male into a female.

Living in the barnacle's shell, the now-female isopod bites into the barnacle and devours its eggs. Male isopods drift by in the sea water and their presence triggers the female isopod to start her own egg production. Unattached males drift close enough to mate with the settled female. Soon, tiny isopods develop inside the new mother. Her body distends with its brood of tiny parasites.

In a final burst of creativity, the female isopod explodes, liberating little males that float away to seek mates of their own. The population explosion that annihilates the mother isopod frees her host barnacle to grow new eggs again. Someday, capricious ocean currents may carry the isopod's descendants back to this rocky site. Then, the acorn barnacles in the neighborhood will face a new invasion by the parasitic pioneers.

HEAT AND SCOURING SAND   Fragile-looking seaweed blades grow on otherwise bare rock adjacent to the barnacles. Some of the seaweeds are adapted to work when they're water-logged and hang dormant when they're dry.

A red alga called nori or laver (*Porphyra* spp.) adjusts its life to tidal interruptions. Soaked by the sea and stoked by sunlight, the soft, pliant sheets of nori work at full speed to make sugar while the sun shines. But as the tide falls, the dark blades dry up and turn crisp as burnt potato chips. Shriveled to a fraction of its weight when wet, the seaweed shuts down its photosynthesis. The nori wraps the rock like shiny, crumpled wrapping paper waiting in suspended animation for the tide's return.

Coarse tufts of the nailbrush alga (*Endocladia muricata*) grow in fuzzy patterns on the rocks. The younger plants are compact and wiry, like scouring pads that hold water inside their woven mesh. The older pads take on bull's-eye patterns from years of grinding work. Waves that convey water to the thirsty seaweeds also carry sand grains that get trapped inside the brush. Then the waves and sand grind away and scour out the centers of the ancient seaweed pads.

Crowded together in tight beds, mussels seal in moisture by clamping their shells tightly closed during low tide.

A MINIATURE ZOO   The wiry pads of seaweeds teem with unseen life. Eggs of marine flies (*Limonia* spp.) cling to the seaweed branches, waiting for their time to hatch. At night, tiny shrimplike amphipods and isopods sneak out from hiding places in the weedy tangle and chew down the surrounding brush.

Just below the wiry weeds, the rocks bloom with more delicate flat blades of nori and the finest threads of red and green algae (*Urospora* and *Bangia* spp.). The marine fly eggs hatch into worm-like larvae that wiggle from the brush. At night, they roam the rocks to gnaw on these seaweed delicacies, leaving behind a bare path where they've crawled.

As the fly larvae grow, they expand their tastes to tougher seaweeds like the wiry nailbrush alga that served as their early homesite and nest. Their larval lives have a spartan focus on finding food and growing up. Metamorphosis transforms the worms into adult flies. In their few short hours of adulthood, marine flies don't eat at all. They survive only long enough to mate and lay their eggs within the seaweed brush.

MUSSEL BEACH   Where waves slap hard against the shore, mussels crowd together in tight colonies. The mussels fix themselves in place by making a wiry glue that hardens into byssal threads—thin attachment lines that hold each shell tight to the rock.

In air, the tiers of dark blue shells are closed and still; in water, they come to life. With their shells slightly open, the mussels rhythmically beat tiny hairs, or cilia, to draw in the sea water rich with the plankton they eat. Inside each mussel, gills filter plankton from the water and then move the feast on to the mussel's mouth.

It's a life of feast or famine. When there's sea water on the mussel bed, the animals keep busy pumping water and sifting food.

Mussels fix themselves in place on the rocks with byssal threads of glue.

The sea water funnels through the maze of shells to the individual animals. Each one does its part to maintain the water movement, filtering two to three quarts of water an hour. When the tide falls and leaves them high and dry, the mussels shut their shells up tight and wait for the sea to return.

TRAILS THROUGH THE BRUSH Snails slide by on homemade trails of slime, past the isolated algal bushes, into the mussel bed and out again. Dainty periwinkles mix with robust black turban snails (*Tegula funebralis*). The youngest turban snails reside high within this zone. As they mature, they gradually migrate down to lower levels, creating a hierarchy of snail sizes on the rocks. Like the periwinkles, turban snails rasp the microscopic film of algae off the rocks as they move. When a decaying pile of drift kelp drapes the shore and turbans chance upon it, they munch on the pungent mass of kelp as they crawl across it.

A group of snails called dogwinkles (*Nucella* spp.) search for meaty meals. A handful of these predators patrol a site that's about four foot square. Even in low densities, they put stress on other populations. If all dogwinkles chose the same kind of prey, they'd wipe out that creature locally. But each individual snail has its own dietary preferences: some concentrate on barnacles; others favor the flavor of slow limpets or whatever prey's most abundant.

Once a dogwinkle selects a barnacle, it boldly pressures it for a meal. The snail nudges apart the plates of the protective door to the barnacle's shell to get to the meat inside. Another dogwinkle attacks a dark blue mussel chosen from a crowded colony of bivalves. This snail uses its tongue to drill into the mussel's shell. When the drill penetrates the shell, the snail rasps away at the mussel's meat. Then the snail slurps up its lunch of ground meat through the fresh hole in the shellfish.

Dogwinkles are predatory snails that attack and eat barnacles and mussels.

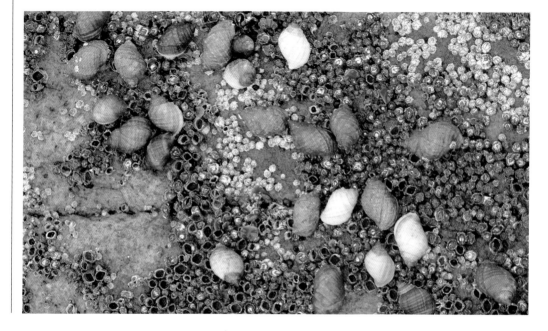

A Scavenger's Picnic As the tide falls from the high intertidal zone, limpets slide under the dripping rockweeds, snails flee to cozy crevices and mussels close up tight. A shore crab (*Pachygrapsus crassipes*) scurries sideways past the mussel patch. When waves threaten to carry it away, the crab backs into a crevice and spreads out its legs to wedge itself in place.

A shore crab hides in tight crevices when not scavenging dead plants and animals on the rocky shore.

Sidestepping smaller wave splashes, the crab confidently scrambles up a rocky slope. Sometimes the crab hunts snails to eat; other times it scavenges dead plants and animals on shore, or harvests a seaweed salad using its large claws to scrape algae off the rocks.

The crab marches to its own internal drummer, adjusting its lively action to the water in its gills. It spends at least half its time in air, drying out as it climbs high up on the rocks. The crab stores sea water near its gills so it can breathe while out of the water. As the crab dries out, its respiration slows. When its internal waters dip too low and need to be replenished, the crab dances sideways down to the tide pools, moistens its gills, then moves back up on the rocks.

Gulls visit rocky shores in search of meals, which may include tough-to-swallow sea stars.

A kelp fly alights on a sunny rock. With a lunge, the crab grabs the fly and pops it in its mouth. The quick meal and hasty movement attracts the attention of other creatures; hungry gulls (*Larus* spp.) spy the crab. In a flash, a gull swoops in and nabs the crab, catching it by one leg. Bird and crab struggle, locked in a momentary battle.

The skirmish ends abruptly when the crab casts off its shackled leg and dives into a crevice. Left holding a single skinny leg, the gull swallows its meager meal, then spreads its wings and flies off in search of other fare.

Out of sight, the crab hides, its body flattened against the walls of the damp crevice. Slowly inching its way down the angled crevice to a tide pool lined with seaweeds, it seeks a haven from the birds while it grows a replacement leg.

4

TIDE POOL TREASURES

As a wave flings fresh sea splash into a tide pool, a shore crab slips from a narrow crevice into this natural oasis. Here it finds a treasure chest of living jewels: jointed coralline algae that look like beaded necklaces, multicolored sea stars, urchins with royal purple spines and majestic giant green anemones (*Anthopleura xanthogrammica*).

Because the tide pool retains sea water at low tide, it shelters defenseless and disarming sea creatures that are vulnerable to drying out. Low tide accentuates the natural chemistry of life forms assembled in the puddle. Rendezvous and sexual encounters take place in the pool when male and female plants and animals are captive in its rocky embrace.

THE UPPER CRUST Crusts of corallines form mosaics of pink and purple fingerprints on the rocks. Fast-growing crusts overgrow slower species and spread across the rocky surfaces like a blush. A slow-moving leather chiton (*Katharina tunicata*) scrapes its way across the crusts, rasping off bits of the coralline algae and tiny diatoms to eat. It doesn't haul around a solid shell; instead it lugs eight plates of armor on its back. The armor is maneuverable and gives the animal flexibility so it can hug the rugged rock more tightly with its foot.

A lined chiton (*Tonicella lineata*) shimmers colors as it rasps away at its coralline algae background. Patterns of pink and purple lines on its eight plates display the colors of its favorite food.

A giant green anemone nestles in a tide pool amid upright, pink coralline algae (below). Two lined chitons graze on rosy-colored crustose coralline algae (right).

Since the day the chiton converted from a tiny larva floating in the plankton to a settled resident on a rosy-colored crust, it's counted on the coralline algae to provide both its home and food.

Working around the chitons, limpets also cruise the corallines, but they bite deeper than the chitons do, leaving scars and scrapes on the pink patina. In places, they eat right through the thin corallines to bare rock.

ROOKPOOL JOHNNIES   A hundred small, slick fishes find harbor in the tide pool. Some venture from the basin at high tide. They follow the advancing water up the rocks, then head back to their tide pool homes as the tide falls.

Bald sculpins and tidepool sculpins (*Oligocottus* spp.) now return from their journeys of exploration. The smaller of these fishes explore the rocks for tiny shrimplike amphipods. The bigger fishes seek slightly larger prey: shrimps, crabs and isopods.

As the tide ebbs, the fishes head unerringly for home. They bypass the other tide pools, heading for the exact one they vacated. A wave conveys the fishes over the rim into the tide pool. Some slide into shallow crevices; others hide among the algae. These fishes have no gas bladders to lighten their load and make them float; their heavy bodies settle to the bottom of the pool.

With mottled colors that match their surroundings, the sculpins lie motionless, unseen. Well camouflaged with spines and fins that enhance their resemblance to seaweeds, they wait out low tide in the safety of their swimming hole.

Upright coralline algae have flexible joints that bend and sway in the water.

A sculpin's spines and fins camouflage it among the seaweeds (left). A clingfish (right) clings to rocks with a special suction-cuplike fin.

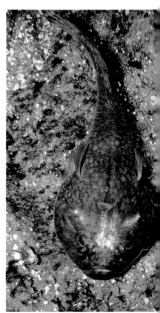

Sculpins aren't the only fishes that call the tide pool home. Northern clingfish (*Gobiesox maeandricus*) use their cuplike pelvic fins like suction cups to cling to boulders in the basin. Slender rockweed gunnels (*Xererpes fucorum*) slip into narrow spaces between rocks. Only their heads expose their hiding places, where their natural lack of buoyancy lets them hold their ground.

A single tide pool can hold dozens of turban snails.

STAR ATTRACTIONS The ochre stars (*Pisaster ochraceus*) that accent tide pools and rocks discharge an aroma into the water. Picking up the scent, brown turban snails (*Tegula brunnea*) quickly scramble from the scene. The voracious sea stars can clean out a tide pool or strip a boulder bare. They pull open mussels, barnacles and other prey stuck to the rocks. Some sea stars take off after moving targets, like the slower snails and chitons that don't flee fast enough from the smell of danger.

The sea stars in turn invite attention from hungry sea otters (*Enhydra lutris*) and birds looking for lunch. Although an otter rarely eats a whole star at one sitting, it can ruin a sea star's shape. A lopsided ochre star in the tide pool shows signs of one such encounter when a sea otter ate one of the sea star's arms and some of its inner organs, then tossed the leftovers aside.

Cast off upside-down and half eaten, the sea star curls its remaining arms beneath it. Hundreds of tiny tube feet on the undersides of its arms clamp down like tiny suction cups against the rock. With a slow and clumsy effort, the star pulls itself against the rock and heaves its body right-side-up. It stretches out its four remaining arms to explore the tide pool using light-sensitive cushions on the tips of its arms to probe for a shady place to hide and recuperate. It locates a shadowy spot under a clump of seaweeds and settles there, gripped tight against the rock. In time, the star will make a brilliant comeback with a regenerated arm.

Next page: An oasis of sea life, the tide pool shelters jewel-like plants and animals that blend in with their riotous background.

A sea star has hundreds of tiny tube feet that act like suction cups to hold it against the rocks.

LIVING LEGACIES

Each mating sea slug is both male and female, and may take turns playing each role.

Reproduction provides living creatures with their links to future natural generations. Many marine organisms have adaptations to improve their odds of reproducing successfully. In the sea, the task of locating a suitable mate is no casual affair.

Most marine animals release their eggs and sperm directly in the sea. The eggs and sperm are probably intact and lively for only a few hours. If they don't link up promptly, the eggs disintegrate or get eaten by other creatures. (And the process of producing them was a waste of the parents' time and energy.)

One solution is for groups of animals to rendezvous at mating time. Some sea stars spawn in unison, each star discharging thousands of sperm or eggs. With luck, they mix together so some of the eggs are fertilized and grow into little stars.

Some fishes, like sculpins, improve their chances for successful sex by preparing attractive nests. Others swim seductive underwater dances or use eye-catching behaviors to attract a mate's attention.

Good timing is more important than a good time; it's the law of the sea. Each male must locate his female counterpart exactly when his sperm is ready and she's ripe with eggs. Some animals rely on cues from the environment, producing eggs or sperm at a certain temperature, or at low tide, or when the days get longer. Others depend on the natural chemistry of the feminine presence. Many male fishes can discharge sperm only when there's a female of their species around.

Birds, barnacles and some fishes join in direct and intimate relationships. In these one-on-one liaisons, the male needs special body parts to transfer sperm to the egg. But animals that brood their eggs or give their young special care usually make fewer eggs and fewer offspring.

Some sea creatures, like strawberry anemones, circumvent the mating game. They make their own companions by chaste but effective methods. These anemones divide in half to clone new, identical versions of themselves.

TABLE MANNERS   Smelling the sea star, turban snails climb the steep walls of the tide pool. One snail loses its grip and tumbles down into the basin. The snail pulls its foot into its shell and closes its trap door tight just before it settles on a giant green anemone. Like a turquoise blossom coming into bloom, the anemone expands from a tightly knotted orb to show its flowery facade. The writhing tentacles that encircle its mouth bear a stunning arsenal. Stinging cells in the anemone's tentacles stun crabs and fishes that stray too close.

The anemone undulates its slippery body until the snail slides right up to the anemone's mouth. Lacking good table manners, the anemone swallows the snail whole. With other prey, like crabs and fishes, the anemone exhibits endless patience. It digests the soft parts of its prey and spits out the hard remains. But the turban snail is safely closed up tight inside its shell. The anemone can't digest the shell or pry open the trap door. Hours later, the anemone spits out the shell. Still safe inside, the turban snail rolls to a low spot in the tide pool.

TIDE POOL THIEVES   Dozens of hermit crabs (*Pagurus* spp.) roam the tide pool, wearing the old shells of dead turban snails. The crabs won't wrestle shells from living turban snails, but they'll fight each other for a proper-sized shell found vacant.

Hermit crab

The hermit crabs scramble on the anemone, immune to its stinging tentacles. Besides the armor offered by their borrowed shells, the crabs wear another line of defense. They steal bits of slime from the anemone and rub it on themselves. This slimy shield offers protection from the anemone's stings.

Anemones use their tentacles to capture small animals to eat.

One hermit crab has outgrown its shell; its body bulges out of its current cover. It needs a bigger shell for a better fit, but the best ones have already been claimed. The hermit crab selects a fellow crab with a larger shell and strikes a threatening pose. With large claws waving, the two crabs spar. One stands to lose its home, but the other in the outgrown shell fights with a special passion. The threatened crab signals defeat. It withdraws its body from the shell and quickly snaps into an empty shell nearby. The victor discards its old, confining casing for the newly won shell. The crab curls its abdomen inside its new shell and uses its back legs to hold the shell on tight. Advancing on its colorfully striped front legs, the hermit crab hauls off its new home and trophy.

Nearby, two hermit crabs strut by together, locked in a tight embrace. This is no squabble over shells; it's the courtship dance of hermit crabs. The male crab totes both his own shell and that of his chosen mate, pausing from time to time to click his shell against hers. Like the effect of castanets on dancers, the rhythmic cadence incites a closer dance. The two crabs extend out of their shells and mate quickly. Within a few seconds, the courtship's over and the male hermit crab scrambles off. The female hermit crab is left with a brood of eggs which she'll carry on her abdomen until they hatch.

A PECULIAR PARTNERSHIP Nearby, a rough keyhole limpet (*Diodora aspera*) plays home base to a scale worm (*Arctonoe vittata*). The worm lives under the limpet's shell tucked between moist folds of flesh where it's sheltered from the extremes of intertidal life. Aligned to face the flow of water, the scale worm curls into position near the limpet's head and copies its host's color. But the imitation isn't its only flattery: the worm will spar with sea stars.

A hermit crab uses an old snail shell to protect its soft, vulnerable abdomen.

When an ochre star stretches out one of its arms to touch the keyhole limpet, the limpet takes a defensive stand, unlike other snails that flee the sea star's squeeze. The limpet raises itself aloft and extends a slippery fold of flesh up over its shell. A secret weapon in the fleshy folds, the scale worm adds to the affront; it chomps down on the tender tube feet of the sea star. Unable to grip its chosen prey, the aggravated star withdraws from the limpet and abandons its attack.

A keyhole limpet reacts to the touch of a predatory sea star by extending a slippery fold of skin over its shell.

A PRICKLY SITUATION   Pink and purple spiny sea urchins (*Strongylocentrotus* spp.) live wedged between rocks in the tide pool. Holding on with hundreds of tube feet, the urchins resist the water's surge. Each wave brings them bits of food that they can catch and eat. Their lower tube feet grip the rock, while their upper ones grab at drifting seaweeds. One urchin catches a loose flap of kelp and transfers it, tube foot to tube foot, to the mouth hidden on its undersides against the rock.

A male urchin cruises the tide pool using its spines like conveyor belts for transportation. Its tiny tube feet stabilize and improve the locomotion. The tubes clamp and release the rock in succession, letting the animal cruise slowly without completely losing its grip. The urchin's mouth rubs the rock, so during any pause in transit, it can scrape off a seaweed snack.

Sea urchins never embrace; at best, their social contacts are superficial. Like sea stars, urchins spawn directly into the sea, so the odds of successful sexual unions seem improbable. Sometimes urchins rendezvous in groups at mating time to spawn simultaneously. The suggestion of nearby sexual activity stimulates them to release their sperm and eggs directly into the sea.

Purple sea urchins bear prickly spines and hundreds of tube feet.

The male sea urchin spurts out a stream of sperm. Nearby urchins sense it and respond by joining in the spree. Female urchins release their eggs; other males discharge more sperm. This orgy in synchrony concentrates urchin eggs and sperm in the tide pool where they're more likely to mix together. It's a long-distance liaison that improves the chances of successful sex.

5

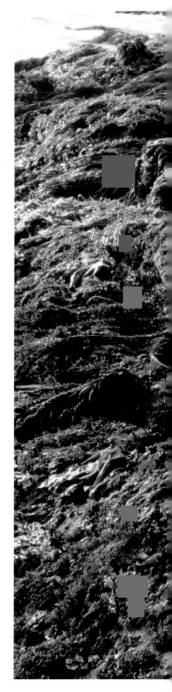

LAND BETWEEN THE TIDES

The middle intertidal zone is truly the land between the tides. Those living in the middle of the tides get the best and worst of both worlds. Seaweeds here grow long and lush in a dozen shapes and colors: purple Turkish towels (*Gigartina* spp.), chartreuse sea lettuce (*Ulva* spp.), iridescent ruby-colored blades (*Iridaea* spp.) and pink crusts of coralline algae. Sea stars, crabs and other creatures live in the dense plant growth. About half the time they're under water, and half the time above it.

When a storm rips up the shore, it leaves vacancies on the rocks where new residents can settle. Twin spores of the red iridescent seaweed claim different niches among the vacancies. One spore settles high on the shore; the other descends at ebb tide, settling on lower rocks.

The spore on the higher perch endures greater turmoil due to the sequence of the tides. For half the day, it's out of water, cut off from its source of nourishment. Without the fertilizers and the moisture it needs to keep up photosynthesis, the plant shuts down at low tide. This interlude of idleness gives *Iridaea* a taste of life on land. Winds dry the plant; rains shock it with fresh water. The sun overheats it and burns it with ultraviolet rays.

To survive in the inferno, the iridescent weed summons every trick at its disposal. With the falling tide, it droops into folds that embrace precious sea water. Internally, the plant makes gels that trap liquid inside. Stressful days in the limelight slow its growth and turn it olive green in color. Perhaps it's not as lovely as the shimmering purple plants below, but these smaller, greener, tougher plants fit their higher calling well enough to stay alive.

The spore that settled lower gets established fast and grows with greater speed. With water almost always around, this *Iridaea* has moisture and a steady source of natural fertilizers to drink in as it needs. Water dims and filters the sunlight that drives its photosynthesis, but enough light penetrates to satiate this purple blade. The steadfast plant works at a routine pace, making sugars at a steady rate. Brighter sunshine on its rubbery blades may reflect a splendid sheen, but it won't speed up production.

Along with seaweeds like *Iridaea*, the middle intertidal is home to thick, muscular snails called abalones that live in bowl-like shells jammed into rocky crevices. Small black abalone (*Haliotis cracherodii*) dwell in crevices, grazing on microscopic algae that coat the rocks. The bigger black abalone grab and gobble kelps that drift within their reach.

Harbor seals often haul out on the weed-cushioned rocks. Long ropes of feather boa kelp and other seaweeds drape the rocks between the tides.

Both large and small abalones depend on the flow of sea water to bring life-giving oxygen. The water circulates under the rim of their shells, over their gills and out through holes atop their shells. On the inside of their shells, the abalones secrete layers of pearly iridescence. These pearl layers offer protection from some of life's most boring irritations: sponges and other animals that drill into abalone shells.

A few of the larger red abalone (*Haliotis rufescens*) hug rocks on the shore. On the outside, their shells are drab with subtle stripes of colors that tell tales of changes in the abalones' diets. Red abalone that eat red algae lay down bands of red color on their shells. Those restricted to a diet of brown algae wear shells with stripes of green or white.

A STINGING ARSENAL   Near the grazing abalones, small elegant anemones (*Anthopleura elegantissima*) decorate a vertical rock wall. Some stand alone in a solitary slouch; others aggregate in dense and squishy beds. As the tide recedes away from them, the anemones retract and shrink down to nearly half their size. Without hard shells or skeletons to support their mushy masses, the anemones seem vulnerable to drying out at low tide. But sticky bumps on their bodies collect sand and bits of shells from other creatures, giving the anemones a protective armor that shields them from some sunlight and helps hold in their moisture.

One of the assembled anemones splits in half to clone itself. The original stretches to divide in two, then the replicas split into four, then eight and so on. Repeated over and over, this act of dividing generates a colony of identical elegant anemones from the same genetic stock.

Sea lettuce (above) and Turkish towel seaweed (right) flourish on rocks. Red abalone (below) graze algae on low rocks.

Aggregating anemones can multiply by dividing in half—one anemone can eventually form a colony of clones.

Nearby, two groups of aggregating anemones from different clones live side by side, but separate. The strip of bare rock between them shows the battle line now drawn. Although they belong to the same species, these anemones are enemies. Each group protects its domain by reaching out to touch someone with specially armed tentacles. Stinging cells in these defending tentacles hold back a competing group, while stinging cells in their other tentacles stun and capture smaller animals to eat.

At the border of one clone, a small anemone confronts a sentry from the other group. Tentacles touching, they exchange a barrage of poison darts. Both warriors are injured in the conflict and they draw away. The combat ends in truce; a demilitarized zone clear of anemones separates the neighboring colonies.

SNAILS IN A STACK   Some animals in the middle intertidal don't fight space wars, they just pick up and move. One of these, a plate limpet (*Notoacmea scutum*), maintains its reputation as the flattest of the limpets. It doesn't have much room under its shell for holding water, so it relies on other adaptations to survive low tide. When the tide starts to fall, the plate limpet heads for lower ground. It crawls down the smooth face of a boulder where sand meets the low part of the rock. Sliding off the rock, the plate limpet burrows down into the sand. There it will stay safely buried until the next high tide comes in.

Most brown turban snails (*Tegula brunnea*) live in deeper waters, but a few join their older cousins, black turban snails, on these intertidal rocks. The venerable black turban snails, some over 30 years old, have retired to this middle tide zone after years in higher, drier places.

A female slipper shell hitches a ride on a turban snail. And a smaller male slipper shell rides on the female's back.

Turban snails transport smaller snails on the backs of their shells. Some carry small limpets that graze microscopic algae off their transportation; others wear slipper snails (*Crepidula adunca*) stacked up in a heap.

The larger, older slipper snails on the bottom of the stack are females. These old girls are sedentary; they don't get out and about much. But even when they're stuck at home in their slippers, these slipper snails attract younger male slipper snails. The females' animal magnetism draws males right to the pile.

Male slipper snails are younger, and smaller, than female snails. They shuffle to the top of the pile to form upper layers on the females and the mixed shells in the stacks. As they age, the males will change to become female slippers. Many of the middle-sized shells in the stack are caught midway in the process of their sex change. They still have both their male and female parts.

SOAKING UP THE BACKSLOSH In the midst of this bustling middle intertidal community, a lumpy black and blue mosaic of mussels alternates with channels of goose barnacles (*Pollicipes polymerus*). In the dense array of bivalves and barnacles, sand and bits of shell accumulate. Scores of worms, six-rayed sea stars and tiny sea cucumbers wiggle in the shell debris. These small animals provide no food in exchange for sharing space since the mussels and goose barnacles filter sea water for their food.

While the acorn barnacles spend their lives in kick-and-recoil feeding frenzies, the goose barnacles take their feeding tempo from the rhythm of the waves. The goose barnacles cluster in the channels and gullies that carry the slosh of waves back to the sea. There they spread out their feathery legs to net plankton from the down-rushing water.

A tightly packed gaggle of goose barnacles provides shelter for scores of smaller creatures.

SLOW SNACKS AND FEEDING FRENZIES

Sea otters use rocks to crack open the shells of clams and other hard-shelled creatures.

Life's a moveable feast on crowded rocks along the shore. Energy to fuel life on the rocks comes from sunlight to plants, then cycles through herbivores to carnivores and finally, scavengers and decomposers.

Photosynthesis forms the foundation of the intertidal food webs. Microscopic phytoplankton drift slowly in the sea or settle down to form a golden felt on pilings, rocks and seaweeds.

Larvae and other tiny animals in the plankton engulf the phytoplankton. They, in turn, are consumed by filter-feeding animals like barnacles and mussels. Turban snails, abalones, sea urchins and other herbivores graze the seaweeds, transforming the plant material into energy to maintain and grow their own bodies.

Some predators make their moves slowly, like the ochre star that uses suction from its tube feet to slowly pull open a small mussel. It slips its stomach inside the bivalve shells, secretes digestive juices and swallows the mussel's liquefied meat.

Sea otters move faster for their meals, grabbing sea urchins, snails and mussels while foraging under water. Back at the surface, an otter floats on its back and uses a rock to crack open the hard shells and get at the meat inside.

Hunched over an animal, a giant sea star uses suction from its tube feet to pry its prey loose.

STARS OF THE MIDDLE Slender sea stars shine in this middle tide zone. Dainty six-rayed stars (*Leptasterias hexactis*) roam the rocks, hunting live prey. By day, they hide in mussel beds or in the jungles of sea lettuce. By night, the stars come out and migrate to the tops of rocks to feed on small snails.

Burdened with heavy loads of eggs and sperm, the dainty six-rayed stars convene a sexual congress. A male star spawns a cloud of sperm; he's quickly joined by other males. Female stars release eggs that collect in sticky lumps.

After their eggs are fertilized, each sea star mother gathers up her brood into a cluster near her mouth, then searches out a rocky crevice where she'll hide out with her young. Humped over her eggs, the female can't flatten out against the rock. She anchors herself as best she can using just the ends of her arms.

The egg lumps block their mothers' mouths. Sea star mothers fast while they fulfill their instinctive maternal duties, going without food for more than a month. They clean the eggs and protect them until the youngsters reach their adult form. When the young stars are developed, they move away to nearby rocks. The mothers stick close by for a few more weeks. Then they leave their two-month-old young to fend for themselves and head off to break their long fast.

Small bat stars (*Asterina miniata*) also live on the rocks here, although larger versions of these flat, webbed stars favor life in

Even though these bat stars are different colors, they're the same species.

deeper waters. Some bat stars are orange, some are creamy beige with orange flecks and a few are purple. They scavenge dead plants and animals along the shore. When they find an appetizing corpse, these stars extend their stomachs to digest their discovery.

FLOWERS IN THE SURF   The surf dishevels the thick mop of surf grass growing on the rocks. Surf grass (*Phyllospadix* spp.) marks the lower limits of the middle intertidal zone. This brilliant green plant is a true flowering plant that survives only in the sea. Its leaves are narrow blades like those of grasses that grow on land, but surf grass rejects a complacent life in soil: its roots seek out harder options. Tenaciously, these roots maintain their grip on submerged rocks in the surf.

Underwater blossoms arranged in twin chains on its resilient spikes confirm this surf grass is no alga. Most of the plants in flower carry female blooms, but a few are male plants bearing pollen. A flood of water from the last high tide released long, sticky strands of pollen from the male flowers. Now, with the falling tide, the pollen drifts with the currents toward another clump of grass. Some of the pollen wraps around a spike of female flowers. When pollinated, these flowers occasionally set seed, then waves and currents spread those few precious kernels to other rocks. But more frequently, the clumps of grass spread by roots and runners to extend the grassy cover on the boulders they have already claimed.

Oxygen bubbles sparkle in this close-up view of bright green surf grass, a flowering plant that grows only in the sea.

6

WET AND WILD

The final, deepest stripe of intertidal life is only exposed to our view once or twice each month. Covered by the sea most of the time, the plants and animals here taste air only during the lowest of low tides.

Most inhabitants of the lush, low zone don't have special adaptations to preserve moisture, since they rarely go uncovered. Instead, seaweeds collapse in layers, and some animals shrivel up during those occasional low tides that leave them high and dry. Some creatures pay the price of losing layers when they dry out, but often it's just the upper parts that die back.

But most of the dangers that creatures face in the low intertidal zone comes from other residents. In this turbulent zone of constant submersion, the plants and animals face an endless war of competition and predation. Despite the liabilities, this territory hosts the richest variety of intertidal life.

SURF GRASS SAFARI   The brilliant surf grass on the boulders dangles down into the lowest intertidal zone. The youngest blades of grass are bright green. Older blades reveal their age by wearing pink polka dots of crustose coralline algae (*Melobesia mediocris*) and dainty scarves of red algae (*Smithora naiadum*).

Orange, red and purple-mottled bat stars advance slowly across the grassy drapes. Two of the stars bump into each other and a gentle brawl begins. Arm over arm, they shove back and forth in a slow-motion skirmish with no apparent winner.

A wave separates the blades of surf grass and exposes other animals. Tunicates are glued on the rock beneath the strips of vegetation. Some are sea squirts that look like light bulbs glowing among the grassy roots; other tunicates form slick colonies.

Each individual tunicate is a saclike animal with two openings to the outside world. The creature feeds by pumping water in one hole, through the netlike gills and out the other hole. As water passes through its gills, small bits of food are trapped in a slime-covered filter. The slimy treat is rolled into a string and passed to the tunicate's mouth.

A bat star extends its translucent stomach out of its mouth to shroud a patch of surf grass. Oozing its digestive juices onto the grass, the star liquifies its lunch, then slurps up the grassy soup. Another bat star spreads its stomach over the tunicates secluded under the curtains of grass. Stuck to the rock, the colony of tunicates can't avoid this acid test. The bat star digests an ample sample of the colony.

Surf grass marks the low intertidal zone that's usually under water. The grass is only exposed by the lowest of tides.

A Multicolored Cloak A multitude of marine plants, from the minute to the majestic, clothe the rocks. The larger seaweeds take on fantasy shapes: red and olive-hued balloons, slender fingers of green velvet and iridescent sapphire mushrooms. In the dim under-water light here, where the rocks are almost always submerged, the seaweeds develop brighter colors. Brown algae parade as golden scarves or leathery ties, and submerged red algae blush with deeper pinks and purples, or glow with blue iridescence.

Luscious-looking sea grapes (*Botryocladia* spp.) persist only in these lowest reaches. The grapelike orbs aren't solid fruits; they're filled with a watery gel that gives the bobbing grapes their buoyancy. Here in the deepest stripe of intertidal life, they're rarely exposed to air—perhaps just a few times a year. During the lowest spring tides, the grapes themselves may shrivel up like raisins or die back from the tips, but their branches and holdfasts usually survive to produce the fruitlike orbs again.

Rosy-red *Rhodymenia* plants spread vegetatively, like creeping shoots of strawberries. The upright red blades develop lower branches that spread out like horizontal runners and attach themselves to the face of the boulder. New blades pop up along these runners, forming red pennants in a series that remains attached to one another.

Between the boulders, golden kelps and long, purple blades flow out with the receding tide. The younger seaweeds are slick and smooth; the older ones bear the tracks of tiny creatures that have settled on them.

Limpets in the Lowest Zone Some animals select one weed for life, like the surfgrass limpet (*Tectura paleacea*) on surf grass and the seaweed limpet (*Discurria insessa*) on feather boa kelp. Old sea-weed limpets orient themselves parallel to the edges of the kelp, while younger ones scatter themselves in arbitrary arrangements. Young and old, the limpets advance up and down the fronds of kelp. They gnaw at the surface as they go—scraping up bits of kelp along with smaller seaweeds growing on the fronds. In places, the limpets munch deep and make depressions in the kelp. When they hunker down in these hollows, the limpets gain some protection against drying out at low tide.

Birds and bat stars (above) scout through the seaweeds for food. Sea grapes and Rhodymenia (below) survive only in the deeper intertidal zones.

Sea grapes

Rhodymenia

Other limpets hitchhike on one kind of seaweed when they're young, then move on to new territory when they're older. A kelp-colored shield limpet (*Lottia pelta*) surfs on a twisting strand of the feather boa kelp. It's at a ripe age for new adventures, so this limpet moves onto a nearby rock. Once settled in its new home, its smooth shell slowly develops ribs and changes to a rocky color.

SPONGE BATHS Gaily colored sponges tint the undersides of rocks in the low intertidal. Overhead, higher rocks are marked by sponges with small violet volcanos (*Haliclona* spp.). In these lower stripes, sponges coat the rocks with bright lemon-yellow crusts (*Aplysina fistularis*) or arch in cream-colored latticeworks (*Leucosolenia eleanor*) or take the shapes of ancient Grecian urns (*Leucilla nuttingi*).

This small pink sea slug, called Hopkin's rose, glides across the rocks on a trail of slime.

A sponge is a simple but efficient animal. Frameworks of spiny spicules support its soft body riddled with canals. The canals are porous passageways that lead to chambers lined with whiplike flagella that drive currents through the sponge. The currents bring oxygen and bits of food into the sponge and carry off its wastes.

Dazzling multicolored sea slugs crawl across the sponges covering the rocks in this zone. These frilly snails without shells sometimes eat the spongy tissue underneath them, prickly spicules and all. Some consume other sea slugs; others gnaw on anemones and take advantage of their prey's unused weapons. After eating an anemone, the sea slug retains its stinging cells. Most sea slugs are poisonous or taste terrible to other animals. The brilliant colors of their bodies may advertise that borrowed stingers and homemade poisons won't improve the taste.

On a bright bed of scarlet sponge (*Ophlitaspongia pennata*), a matching red sea slug (*Rostanga pulchra*) secretes a lovely spiral ribbon. The transparent ribbon is a long egg case that holds about 10,000 scarlet eggs. At first, the eggs match their spongy background perfectly, but they'll fade a bit as they develop.

The adult sea slug has done its work; now it moves on to redder pastures. That sponge-encrusted ledge has been the sea slug's home all its adult life. The sea slug selected it by smell when it left the life of a drifting larva. The slug locates another sponge—another home—by smell. Gliding on a trail of slime, the sea slug heads off in that direction.

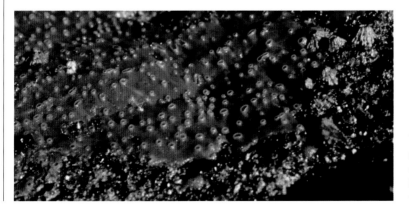

The violet volcano sponge is a simple animal that filters bits of food from the water around it.

FUZZY DISGUISE On nearly every surface here, colonies of moss animals, or bryozoans, make fuzzy coverings on rocks, kelps, even the backs of crabs. The tiny bryozoans grow as fine as cat's hair, but each is a delicate animal with a crystal skeleton for support. Tentacles on the bryozoans filter bits of plankton and bacteria from the water.

On the rocks, the bryozoan fuzz and ostrich-plume hydroids (*Aglaophenia* spp.) form a miniature forest where skeleton shrimp (*Caprella* spp.) and sea spiders (*Pycnogonum* spp.) hide. Long, narrow skeleton shrimp bend and stretch to climb through their tiny jungle. The shrimp use their hooked claws to hang on tight to the hydroids' branches.

A male sea spider prowls the hydroid forest, bearing a huge lump of eggs nearly its own size. Each of its eight long legs ends in a hook. Crawling up another hydroid, the sea spider inserts its mouth into a branch and sucks out a liquid meal.

The fuzzy growth of bryozoans also provides camouflage for larger animals. A decorator crab (*Loxorhynchus crispatus*) wears a coat of moss animals and tiny seaweeds as part of its disguise. The fuzz grows right on the crab but its camouflage is no accident. The crab selects algal fragments and small moss animals from around its habitat and fastens them to dainty hooks on the back of its shell. When the crab sits motionless, it disappears against the background of fuzzy rocks. As long as the crab stays in the neighborhood, it blends in and looks at home.

Many of the dazzling sea slugs eat stinging sea anemones and hydroids (top). A ferocious predatory sea spider crawls across an orange sponge (above).

SINGLE PARENTHOOD Proliferating anemones (*Epiactis prolifera*) in the low tide zone flaunt a rich, if revolutionary, sex life. The small and younger anemones are females. As they grow in size, they grow male organs too. In a proliferating population, the oldest, largest members are hermaphrodites—both male and female at the same time.

Proliferating anemones bear broods of young anemones on their columns.

Older anemones set their own style of reproduction. One may use its own sperm to fertilize its eggs; another may use sperm from some other individual. The inbreeding anemone that provides both eggs and sperm ends up as both mother and father to its brood.

The young anemones who are solely female must fertilize their eggs with sperm from older anemones. Females keep their eggs inside their guts and siphon in sperm to fertilize their eggs. As the fertilized eggs start to develop, they're evicted from their mother. The anemone transfers its offspring out through its mouth and down onto its fleshy "skirt."

Some prolific matriarchs support as many as 30 youngsters on their columns. They don't baby their babies or even provide food for them, but the adults' strong stinging cells may offer some security until the young anemones are more independent.

HIDDEN PLEASURES The undersides of boulders and narrow cracks in the rocks hide fragile brittle stars, wriggling worms and other creatures that turn confinement to an advantage. Delicate flatworms (*Pseudoceros* spp.) swim out to look for sea slugs or other food. The undulating movement of the ruffled edges of their bodies carry them from the dark recesses of the rocks.

Ribbon worms striped with bands of orange, green or purple build mucus tubes to live in, while feather duster worms withdraw into the protection of their upright leathery tubes.

Tiny brittle stars (*Amphipholis* spp.) hide under rocks and in their crevices. Rowing their long arms across the rocks, they slither out of hiding and move out to search for food. Sometimes they catch and eat small animals they come across in their travels. At other times, they make a meal of the mucky wastes of other creatures. A spiny brittle star (*Ophiothrix spiculata*) in a crevice will use one arm to anchor itself and project its other four arms out in the water to catch bits of food on its sticky spines.

Wider crevices hold sea urchins, rock crabs (*Cancer antennarius*) and sea cucumbers. Purple sea urchins sometimes grind out their own holes, using their spines and teeth to slowly burrow into soft rock. Because they grow as they dig, they sometimes become trapped in their caves, growing too big to fit back through the entrance.

An orange sea cucumber (*Cucumaria miniata*) nestles between two rocks in a U-shape, with both its ends toward the moving water. Mucus on the frilly tentacles around its mouth traps bits of food from the sea. With a finger-licking gesture, the sea cucumber draws each tentacle up to its mouth and, one by one, licks them clean.

Small brittle stars with long arms (top) and rock crabs that could reach six inches across (above) hide under boulders and in rocky crevices.

BRILLIANT TREASURES Larger sea stars and predatory snails that usually live in the kelp forest occasionally climb into the lowest stripes of life on rocky shores. As they advance to the lower reaches of the tides, they motivate their prey to move too, up into higher, safer zones.

A huge purple sunflower star (*Pycnopodia helianthoides*) demonstrates its repulsive powers of persuasion as it climbs the boulder. Its 24 arms coordinate the synchrony: 15,000 tube feet holding on, then letting go, in rapid sequence. Pincers on the star's back seize a bit of sea cucumber flesh when the star brushes against it. The sea cucumber shrinks back into its crevice home, out of harm's way.

Purple sea urchins sense the nearby sea star. Those trapped in holes writhe in their prisons. The sea urchins that are unrestrained flee from the terror. One shoves another off the rock as it escapes. The sunflower star humps over the dislodged urchin and engulfs it. Hours later, when the star moves away, only a pile of dislodged spines and the hollow test that was the urchin's shell remain.

Sunflower stars usually live in deeper water, but occasionally they climb up on the rocky shore in search of prey.

COASTAL CONNECTIONS

On rocky shores, tides and waves extend a critical connection to other habitats. At high tide, as each wave comes and goes, water surges over and between the rocks. The currents carry spores and larvae away from the rocky shore and sweep them out to sea.

The drifting spores and larvae pass through other habitats on their journey. Some linger in the kelp forests; others are swept to the sandy seafloor where they're sucked in by hungry clams and burrowing anemones. Most drifters perish at sea. But a few return to shore where they may colonize new territories.

Without its watery connections with other habitats, the rocky shore community would smother or starve. The swirling sea dilutes the droppings of the animals stuck on the shore that could not otherwise dispose of their wastes for themselves. Waves prune dead and dying branches off the seaweeds and transport the branches to another spot. And while the water sometimes sweeps life's natural litter from the rocks, just as often it drapes the shore with debris from deeper reefs and other habitats.

The sea provides the lively link of food from other marine habitats. Waves bring food and oxygen to the animals and plants on the rocky shore. When the tide comes in and covers the plants and animals with water, their table's set, the feast can start.

CONNECTIONS WITH THE KELP FOREST A hundred yards from shore, a forest of giant kelp (*Macrocystis pyrifera*) rises up from its rocky foundation. About 30 feet below the surface, the kelps' rootlike holdfasts secure them to the rocks. Buoyed by gas-filled floats, the kelp stipes rise like anchor lines from the seafloor to the surface. The golden kelp blades spread out across the water's surface to form the forest canopy.

Sea otters doze in the canopy, wrapped in the kelp fronds that keep them from drifting off during their naps. Below the golden canopy, a rich community of plants and animals thrives in the undersea forest. Harbor seals and sea otters dive in the forest to hunt for prey.

Kelp surfperch (*Brachyistius frenatus*) hide out between the kelp blades; turban snails slowly glide up and down the stipes. Hundreds of rockfishes (*Sebastes* spp.) make their homes in the forest. Some use their swimbladders to regulate their buoyancy, hovering in midwater between the towering kelps. Other rockfishes dwell at the bottom of the forest, stationed on rocks with snails, abalones and other creatures of the forest floor.

Seabirds flock to rocky shores to roost and rest, providing a link between the air, shore and sea.

Heermann's gull

Western gull in breeding plumage

The framework of the forest modifies the flow of water through it. The waters slow down as they pass through the canopy and between the fronds of kelp. An offshore current carries drifting larvae from the rocky shore. The larvae must pass through the forests twice: first on their journey out to sea, then on their way back in to shore.

The slower pace between the kelp fronds extends their sojourn in the forest, where the larvae face a greater risk of meeting up with danger. They look like swarms of gourmet samples to the fishes of the forest. Tiny rockfishes gobble up the larvae, then they, in turn, become food for larger rockfishes.

Many larvae never reach the open sea; others make the outward trip only to perish on the way back. But a few hardy and lucky larvae make it through the forest's filter. These find their way back to the rocky shore and settle down to live there.

Traffic between rocky shores and kelp forests is not a one-way shuttle. Creatures from the forests sometimes relocate to the near-shore rocks. Winter storms rip the giant kelp plants from the forest and set them adrift. Some drift to shore with hundred of animals still in their holdfasts. Huge mounds of kelp fronds and holdfasts snag the rocks and drape the shore.

Harbor seals (*Phoca vitulina*) and other pinnipeds are tied to shore at certain times in their lives. They mate and give birth on the intertidal rocks; they also beach themselves to rest. Taking a break from fishing, the seals scoot up onto the rocks as the tide falls. On route to a sunny resting spot, they flatten seaweeds and squash some creatures on the rocks. At low tide, they're napping well above the water, balanced on the tops of boulders like fat sausages.

Animals on the rocky shore release larvae that drift through the kelp forest on their way out to sea (top). Harbor seals haul out on the rocky shore to rest and warm themselves (above).

BETWEEN PACIFIC TIDES

Over the past century, thousands of novice biologists have come to Monterey Bay for their first taste of intertidal science. Students come from Hopkins Marine Station, Moss Landing Marine Laboratories, Long Marine Laboratory and other institutions of higher learning. They scramble over slippery rocks with buckets and thermometers or stick their heads right into the water to watch and learn about the world between the tides. Each year a new set of young biologists arrives full of questions and curiosity about the ocean.

Ed Ricketts was one such biologist who came to Monterey in the 1920s to live and learn about the bay. As partner in a biological supply business, Ricketts spent long hours on intertidal rocks, observing, collecting and developing ideas about the processes that determine where creatures live on those rocky shores.

He served as inspiration for the character Doc in John Steinbeck's book *Cannery Row*. But Rickett's great contribution to biology is his book *Between Pacific Tides* which summarizes his careful observations and perceptions about life between the tides.

After years of observation and study, Ed Ricketts summarized his work on the intertidal zonation of marine animals and plants in the book, Between Pacific Tides.

A Union with the Open Sea Cold coastal water rich with larvae moves offshore where it encounters warmer oceanic currents. Face to face, the currents meet. The sea's surface wears a supple belt that marks this line of convergence. Creatures from the two habitats collect at the front. Drifting larvae and spores from shore mingle with larger drifters from the ocean.

Pulsing translucent jellyfishes and iridescent comb jellies from the open sea make a picnic of the scene, engulfing some of the teeming larvae. A drifting log bobs by. This flotsam carries pelagic goose barnacles (*Lepas anatifera*). Although they can't float alone, the barnacles thrive on the open sea. Their long, flexible body parts reach out into the water. With parted shells, their feathery legs grab at the larvae in the water.

The offshore winds die down; the cooler water—still rich with larvae—moves back in toward shore. Eventually some of the tiny creatures make their way to another shoreline with a new array of rocks. The sea floods the most seaward rocks first. Many of the tiny drifting animals and spores bail out here, at the first opening they get. Some wait and settle on rocks closer to shore. Others contribute to life on the rocky shore in old, familiar ways, becoming bits of food for barnacles and other filter-feeding animals.

Air, Land and Sea Seabirds fill the sky above the rocky shore: pelicans, gulls, terns, cormorants and other flying visitors. Tied to land for nesting and to the sea for food, their antics in the salt air are visual links to land and sea as they swoop and plummet from the sky. The birds bring remnants of their offshore feasts back to shore: their wastes coat the rocks with guano. And when seabirds die on shore, their bodies provide food for rock crabs and other scavengers.

A Brandt's cormorant (*Phalacrocorax penicillatus*) flies out from the rocky shore to the open coastal waters. Looking like a skinny black sea crow, it's superbly skilled at fishing. Unlike other diving birds, it has no natural oils to keep the cold sea water from stealing its body heat. Its feathers soak up sea water, which helps this bird sink like a stone, but the advantage comes at a cost: exposure to the cold burns calories quickly, so the bird has to catch more food.

The cormorant plunges into the sea and kicks 30 feet down to nab a squid. Another dive nets a mouthful of anchovies. The cormorant must eat more than its body weight each day, just to maintain itself. Raising young cormorant chicks requires even more food and energy.

Full of fish, the cormorant flies back to shore. It lands on a boulder and stretches its wing to dry in the sun. With a splat, the bird squirts out its wastes in an explosive spurt. The fresh guano, rich in nitrogen, adds to the ancient white layers from other seabird droppings.

Dry and warm again, the cormorant soars off to collect nesting material. A dive near shore provides red seaweeds for the nest; a brief flight inland contributes branches and leaves from land. The cormorant flutters back to shore and arranges the pile into a nest.

An American oyster-catcher probes the seashore for a tasty shellfish meal (below). Adult and juvenile pelicans perch together on a rock marked by smears of white guano (bottom).

DEEPER WATERS Where cold water wells up from the ocean depths, it brings natural riches to the surface. Currents deliver these natural fertilizers to the rocky shore where they enrich the multicolored seaweeds growing on the rocks. Urchins, snails and other creatures on the rocks use the weeds for double duty: they hide under the drapes and scrape some algae off for food.

Some fishes come up from deeper habitats to use the rocky shore to their advantage. Lingcod (*Ophiodon elongatus*) migrate from habitats 900 feet deep to lay their eggs on nearshore rocks. When females head back down to the depths, male lingcods near shore stay to guard their nests until the eggs hatch.

Storms rip seaweeds off the rocks and carry the debris away from shore. Light weeds float on the surface, but denser, heavier seaweeds sink to the seafloor. Currents carry the dense drifting masses down into deeper waters. Deep sea animals take advantage of their windfall. Deep sea urchins (*Allocentrotus fragilis*) that live in deep sea canyons picnic on the feast from above.

LINKS WITH LAND Along rocky coasts, the narrow strip of intertidal life is delicate property. This meeting place of air, land and sea faces endless assaults and invasions. Some are natural events that change the face of the community. Storm waves beat against the shore and cull weak or sickly creatures from their home sites. Uprooted trees and drifting logs crash against the rocks and clear off bare space where new arrivals can settle.

Even those of us who love the sea can pose a threat to precious life there. A careless scramble on intertidal rocks can crush and smother unseen creatures. An overturned rock exposes its hidden creatures to unnecessary dangers: predators may detect their hiding places or they may perish simply from drying out.

Live gently on the earth; respect the sea. Low tides offer us a peek at the treasures in the tide pools, but the rocky coast remains a fragile wilderness to be protected.

Careful and considerate tide pool scholars observe marine creatures in their habitats and leave nature as they found it.

INDEX